PRIMATES

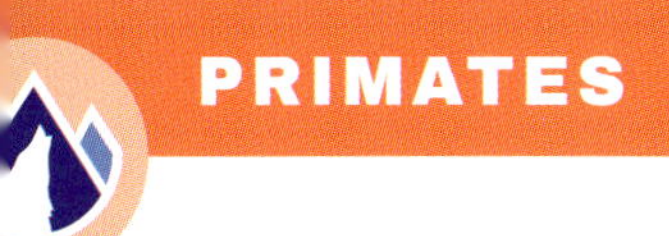

GIBBONS

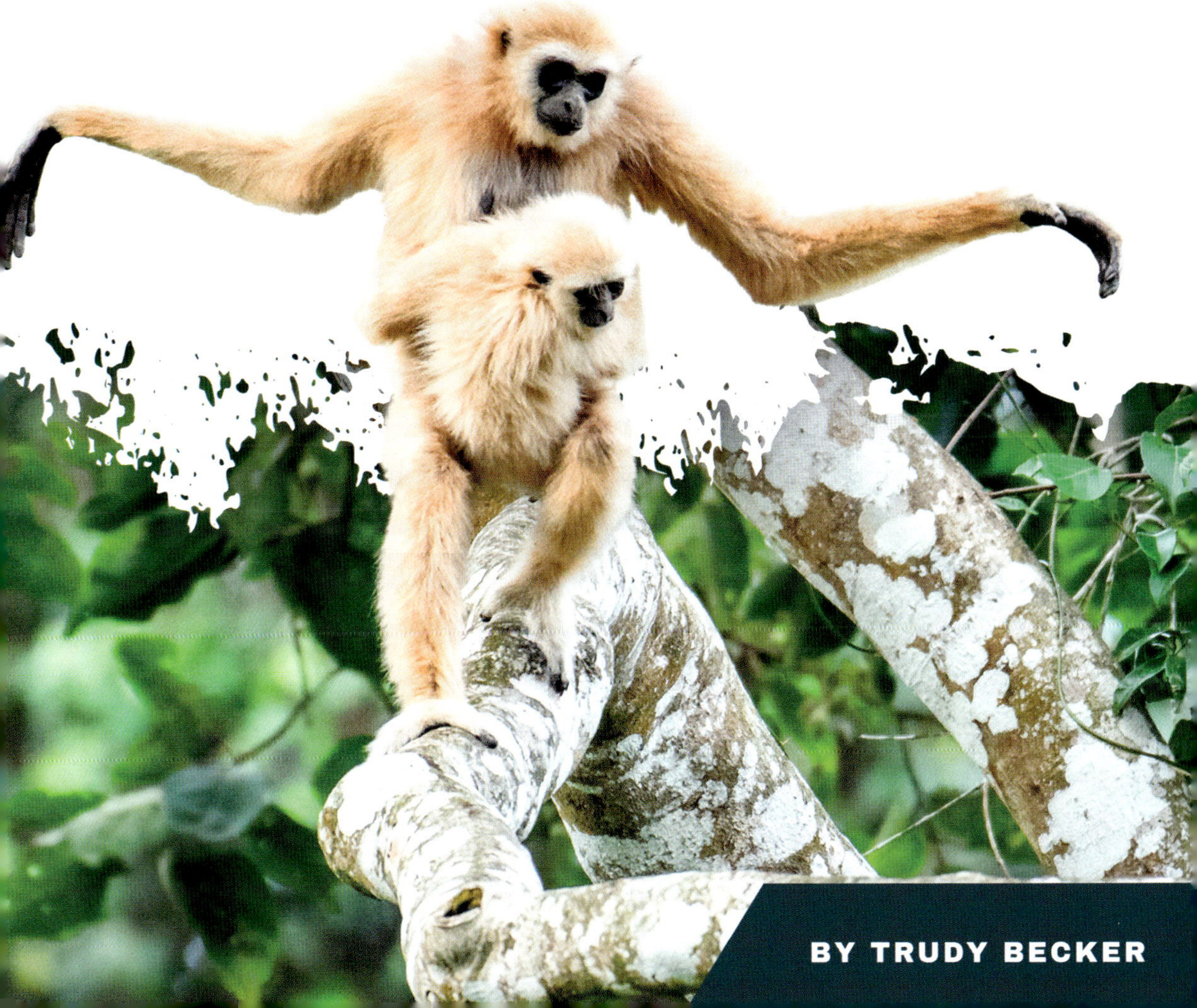

BY TRUDY BECKER

WWW.APEXEDITIONS.COM

Apex is distributed by North Star Editions:
sales@northstareditions.com | 888-417-0195

Produced for Apex by Red Line Editorial.

Photographs ©: Shutterstock Images, cover, 1, 4–5,6–7, 9, 10–11, 12–13, 15, 16–17, 18, 19, 20–21, 24, 29; iStockphoto, 14, 22–23, 26–27

Library of Congress Control Number: 2025939162

ISBN
979-8-89250-795-0 (hardcover)
979-8-89250-824-7 (paperback)
979-8-89250-880-3 (ebook pdf)
979-8-89250-853-7 (hosted ebook)

Printed in the United States of America
Mankato, MN
012026

NOTE TO PARENTS AND EDUCATORS

Apex books are designed to build literacy skills in striving readers. Exciting, high-interest content attracts and holds readers' attention. The text is carefully leveled to allow students to achieve success quickly. Additional features, such as bolded glossary words for difficult terms, help build comprehension.

CHAPTER 1

FOREST DUET

It is a warm day in the forest in Vietnam. Two gibbons rest in the trees. The male gibbon swings to a higher branch. The female follows him.

Gibbons can leap more than 50 feet (15 m) between branches.

Next, the gibbons start singing. The male makes a whooping call. The female answers. Their sounds ring through the air.

Female gibbons tend to sing long notes. Males tend to grunt and whistle during songs.

The gibbons' voices rise and fall. Some sounds are low booms. Others are fast and high. Each sound adds to the song.

LOUD SOUNDS

Some types of gibbons have throat sacs. Gibbons use these body parts to sing. The sacs fill with air. They make the gibbons' songs louder.

Siamangs are a type of gibbon. Their throat sacs can stretch to be as big as their heads.

CHAPTER 2

ALL ABOUT GIBBONS

Gibbons are small **primates**. There are around 20 different gibbon **species**. Most weigh between 12 and 17 pounds (5 and 8 kg).

Most gibbons grow between 16 and 26 inches (40 and 65 cm) tall.

Gibbons have long arms and strong legs. They can cling tightly to branches. They often swing from tree to tree.

A gibbon's arms are usually 1.5 times longer than its legs.

FAST FACT

Gibbons can move up to 35 miles per hour (56 km/h) when swinging between branches.

Yellow-cheeked gibbons live in the rainforests of Vietnam, Laos, and Cambodia.

Gibbons live in southern Asia. Most are found in tropical rainforests. These areas are warm and wet. Gibbons live in countries such as India, Thailand, and China.

LOSING LAND

Many gibbons are losing their **habitats**. People cut down rainforests. Then they use the land to make palm oil. As a result, many gibbon species are **endangered**.

People have cut down many trees to clear land for palm oil farms.

CHAPTER 3

LIFE IN THE WILD

Gibbons spend most of their lives in the forest **canopy**. They sleep and eat there. They rarely touch the ground.

When gibbons walk on branches, they hold out their arms for balance.

Gibbons can spend up to nine hours each day searching for food.

Gibbons eat mostly fruit. But they also eat other plant parts, such as shoots and leaves. Gibbons search for food during the day. At night, they curl up between branches to sleep.

Gibbons have pads on their rumps that help them stay comfortable while resting in trees.

A gibbon group's area often covers 50 to 125 acres (20 to 50 ha).

Gibbons live in small family groups. Each group has its own territory. Gibbons usually stay in that area for many years.

SING-OFF

Each group of gibbons **defends** its area. But groups rarely fight. Instead, gibbons sing on their land to show they control it. Nearby groups hear the calls and stay away.

CHAPTER 4

LIFE CYCLE

Most gibbon groups include a male, a female, and their babies. The male and female are **mates**. Females have one baby every few years.

Some gibbons stay with the same mate for life.

Gibbons are born tiny and helpless. Babies cling to their mothers and drink their milk. But over time, they learn and grow. Parents teach them how to survive.

LOTS OF LEARNING

For the first year, a baby gibbon relies on its mother completely. The mother feeds it and carries it around. After that, the baby can move and find food on its own.

◀ **A baby gibbon holds tightly to its mother's fur for the first several months.**

Gibbons stay with their families until about they are eight years old. Then, they go off to start families of their own.

Gibbons can live
for 25 to 35 years
in the wild.

COMPREHENSION QUESTIONS

Write your answers on a separate piece of paper.

1. Write a few sentences explaining the main ideas of Chapter 2.

2. What sounds would you make to show your bond with someone?

3. What do baby gibbons eat?

- **A.** fruit
- **B.** milk
- **C.** seeds

4. What might happen if gibbons keep losing their habitats?

- **A.** There would be fewer gibbons.
- **B.** There would be more gibbons.
- **C.** There would be more rainforests.

5. What does **territory** mean in this book?

Gibbons live in small family groups. Each group has its own ***territory****. Gibbons usually stay in that area for many years.*

- **A.** things that gibbons smell
- **B.** places where gibbons live
- **C.** sounds that gibbons make

6. What does **relies** mean in this book?

For the first year, a baby gibbon ***relies*** *on its mother completely. The mother feeds it and carries it around.*

- **A.** needs and depends
- **B.** swings and falls
- **C.** jumps and climbs

Answer key on page 32.

GLOSSARY

bond

A close relationship.

canopy

A dense layer of leaves and branches high up in trees.

defends

Keeps others out of an area.

endangered

In danger of dying out forever.

habitats

The places where animals normally live.

mates

Pairs of animals that come together to have babies.

primates

Animals in a group that includes apes and monkeys.

species

Groups of animals or plants that are similar and can breed with one another.

TO LEARN MORE

BOOKS

Kington, Emily. *Habitat Destruction*. Hungry Tomato, 2022.

Murray, Julie. *Fun Facts About Monkeys*. Abdo Publishing, 2022.

Rains, Dalton. *Chimpanzees*. Apex Editions, 2025.

ONLINE RESOURCES

Visit **www.apexeditions.com** to find links and resources related to this title.

ABOUT THE AUTHOR

Trudy Becker lives in Minneapolis, Minnesota. She likes exploring new places and loves anything involving books.

INDEX

ANSWER KEY:
1. Answers will vary; 2. Answers will vary; 3. B; 4. A; 5. B; 6. A